BRUSH AND HORIZON

Your Complete Handbook for

Seascape Masterpieces

Tiffany Jesse

Table of Contents

CHAPTER ONE

INTRODUCTION

How to Paint a Seascape Step by Step In this article, I'll show you how to paint a seascape using close-up light, a harsh shore, and a breaking wave in the best possible way. It is a madly troublesome subject to Paint seascapes. Breaking waves, ocean showers, surf, light, shakes, and disturbing cools are shocking upgrades for a shocking seascape painting. Regardless of the way that acrylics could be used to paint this ideal show-stopper, oils were used to make this pearl. Structure In this masterpiece, the plan is coordinated looking like an "S," and the direct between the stones in the forward locale causes to see the sensible breaking wave. The breaking wave is the central area of interest in the imaginative creation.

The "S" connection suggests that there is a beat in the imaginative creation.

COLORS I used oil paint to paint this work of art and the colors I used are as follows:

1. Titanium white

2. Drank sienna

3. A yellow ochre is cadmium yellow

4. Red cadmium

5. Alizarin red

6. Ultramarine blue

7. Coming up next is a quick layout of the Thalo green brushes I used to make this convincing work in regards to craftsmanship:

• No.5 level

• No.3 level

• No.2 level

• No.3 filbert

• No.1 round

• No.0 round

STAGE 1: Demoralizing INTO THE Innovative Joint effort Drawing THE

Improvement I'm painting on a material board that is 8 jerks by 8 inches. The material is an oil-made medium weave that is mounted to Baltic birch. I framed the blueprint using a №1 round brush and consumed sienna mixed in with Liquin Novel (Liquin). I'm utilizing liquid to thin the paint, which has the additional advantage of accelerating the drying system. During the most widely recognized approach to destroying, I use free painterly brush draws as well as No. 5 and No. 3 level brushes everywhere.

PAINTING THE DARK CREDITS

When I begin a painting, I immediately notice the scene's overall dullness. Respect exhibits a subject's sensitivity or absence of definition; we will find our most lovely lights and haziest shadows in the scene's genuine front. In any case, as landforms retreat into the distance, the worth scale limits, dull properties and lights become less recognizable. You can quickly create a noticeable dynamic by first arranging the dark features and shadows, making it much easier to comparatively paint the locations in light. I start by applying a mix of titanium white, consumed sienna, ultramarine blue, and a humble amount of alizarin red to the cloud shadows. This seascape's haziest elements are the stones' shadows, particularly as demonstrated by a nearer viewpoint. Using a mix of consumed sienna and ultramarine blue, I paint the stone shadows.

PAINTING THE SKY AND FOGS

Since I have separate in the goliath areas of shadows, I begin painting the district in light, starting from the establishment and working forward. The fogs were painted with titanium white and a little consumed sienna. The sky is a mix of ultramarine blue, titanium white, and a little thalo green.

I paint the sea and waves with changing mixes of ultramarine blue, titanium white, thalo green, and yellow ochre. The wave's sensible district is a blend of yellow ochre, titanium white, and thalo green. For the shadowed areas of water and froth, I utilized various mixes of ultramarine blue, finished sienna, titanium white, and alizarin dull red.

PAINTING THE STONES AND OCEAN

I added more tone to the stones and painted the reflected light on the stone surfaces. Since the water is collapsing over the mirrored light, it has a blue tone to it. I use a mix of titanium white, consumed sienna, ultramarine blue, and alizarin dull red for the stones. In the front water and hazes, I have nearly elucidated these Tanta mount tones, which will sort out these zones and select mix organizing inside the material. A blend of drank sienna and titanium white was used to paint the parts of the breaking waves and the white water. I'm keeping the game plan's worth really covered to anger the issues when I add the last parts after the work has been finished.

PAINTING LIGHT

In a difficult situation I paint the locale of the stones that are in full sunshine. I joined consumed sienna, titanium white with a bit of ultramarine blue, and alizarin ruby for the stones on the left. I have blended consumed sienna, yellow ochre, ultramarine blue, and titanium white to make different rocks.

STAGE 2: ADDING Nuances AND REFINING THE Material. Right when the material was dry I began adding nuances to it. I at long last use filbert and No3 level brushes, which are additional genuine brushes. To give the clouds, foam, and white water more depth, I combined titanium white with a small amount of dazed sienna, ultramarine blue, and alizarin ruby. I'm keeping the collections worth a little lower by postponing my lightest characteristics for the rest of the material. I paint more nuances in the water by adding waves and foam plans toward the front. Here, I'm entering the appearance stage, where I'm directing the different creation plans. On the left half of the craftsmanship, I added nuances, outlined the stones, hardened the breaks, and painted a few features on the sunlit stone surfaces.

STAGE 3: Yet again last Subtleties Since it is as yet being hand tailored, I let it dry prior to adding the last subtleties. I paint highlights on the breaking waves and white water using a mix of titanium white with a sprinkle of yellow ochre. Only a negligible portion of the components is used to genuinely revive the waves. Precisely when I paint the stones with features, I utilize this comparative blend. I add the foam guides for the waves with a blend of ultramarine blue, titanium white, and a little alizarin red to complete the material. Subsequently, a mix that is near an assortment is utilized to cover the waves and spills up the stones. I have been painting seascapes for a surprisingly long time considering the way that I value painting the ocean. If you value craftsmanship and want to learn more about painting seascapes, you might want to check out this blog section, which lists the best locations in my gathering cycle. Stay tuned because I will participate in additional content shows on my blog that will reveal the best way to fan out scenes and seascapes. In this bit by bit material show I will let you know the best structure for painting this seascape of the wild sea as shown in the picture under. This seascape relies on the wild sea at Piha Sea side worked with in West Auckland, New Zealand. Coordinating Made by Workmanship to really make a seascape that legitimizes itself, we need to design our image so we can find what is going on with the handicraft. Unambiguously organized central fixations and persuading use concerning gathering to spread out environment and space inside made by craftsmanship can accomplish importance in a work. I shut what parts I needed in the scene and where I stayed aware of my veritable indication of social event to relate the record of this material. I accumulated a lot of pencil expects to design the piece before I even started coordinating this image so I could see what could work and what wouldn't. This is essential for ensure that I won't have any issues there of brain while figuring out the picture with creation gives. I'm ceaselessly amazing my own shortcoming to figure out the annoying subject of creation. I consistently adhere to two or three crucial standards to reduce the likelihood of encountering relationship issues while painting. Avoid the going with considering the way that they might actually steamed the equilibrium of the piece:

• **Center Lines:** This could be a critical compositional issue that causes us issues we didn't anticipate. For instance, meaning the spot of relationship of the work with a mix carving or painting the sea's outlook line in material so the distance between the sea and sky is nearly something basically the same. The synthesis develops long because of these consistent issues! To make strain in the convincing craftsmanship, I painted a lower horizon line and set the nature of association, the unmistakable breaking wave, aside of obsession.

• **Mixtures:** There are occasions of dull parts, plans, and shapes that can disturb the synthesis' concordance while painting rocks that are overall of a for all intents and purposes unclear size and shape. Your ideal pearl's deviations might be endeavoring to pull out notwithstanding, when you have started your image. It's perfect to sporadically have a second arrangement of eyes investigate your business.

• **Painting in the Corners:** Yet again considering the way that our thought is quickly drawn to the corner, serious areas of strength for painting, shapes in the corners can lose an especially arranged plan. Guarantee anything that you paint toward the side of the material blends in and works with the rest of the imaginative creation, generally speaking. Overcomplicating the inventive stream: With parts, plans, and shapes that match, it is reasonable to have a remarkable game plan happening right now in a piece of craftsmanship. This makes the agreement look bewildered and makes it chasing after for the eye to figure out where to look. To diminish this bet of over tangling your creation it is ideal to pick what your particularly regular for plot will be and work in parts around that. I made the breaking wave the standard object of interest and mark of association in this artistic creation. The possibility of relationship of the synthesis is the wild sea especially the breaking waves in the forward looking locale, yet I other than expected to set 'Lion Rock' which is a respected achievement of Piha Sea side. I painted Lion Rock on the right half of the persuading work regarding craftsmanship considering how the accomplishment is so monster. Anyway, this could suggest that the creative outcome is out of harmony. To conclude this issue and make the imaginative creation more fluid, I added the two rocks in the forward locale to find the affiliation and direct the eye toward the obvious breaking wave. In addition, I moved the ability to assemble to the side of the material. Moreover, the fogs in the material's upper left half have made. You know that the message "actually take a look at me" ought to be conveyed by your place of connection, and it ought to have supporting components that cause to notice this reality. I painted this seascape on material with oils for My Appearance. The imaginative piece is 20 by 24 by 610 by 500 millimeters in size. To paint this scene, I have used Lang.

TOP OF THE LINE OIL PAINTS

• Titanium white • Cadmium yellow • Cadmium yellow huge • Yellow oxide • Consumed sienna • Consumed umber • Cadmium red light • Quinacridone maroon • Ultramarine blue • Pthalo blue • Cobalt blue • Cobalt greenish blue • Pthalo green I likewise utilized the medium Liquin Novel, which controls the advancement of the paint and rates up the drying time.

CHAPTER TWO

MANUAL FOR PAINTING THE SEASCAPE

Stage 1: Before beginning this show-stopper, I coordinated the materials by covering them with a layer of consumed sienna. When consumed sienna is added, it unmistakably warms the entire material and gives the piece a distinct quality by passing through the paint layers. You can as such use consumed umber. To set up the material with the consumed sienna layer I mixed consumed sienna in with liquin and thinners. I then applied it to the material with a large hake brush, attempting to apply the mix in a thin layer. Preceding beginning a new development, I let it dry for a couple of days when in doubt. I have framed the scene with consumed umber mixed in with liquin.

Stage 2: As I begin upsetting in the creation I have started painting the sky which sets the overall scene for made by craftsmanship. I will use the sky to compare my reasonable qualities to the rest of the craftsmanship. The blue of the open sky is mixed in with a blend of cobalt blue, cobalt blue-green and titanium white. You can also use turquoise light as an alternative to cobalt greenish blue. I have painted the parts of the fogs using titanium white. I have in like manner fired concealing the hazes the skyline, which I acknowledge should appear far away. I have combined titanium white with de-splashed assortments with ultramarine blue, consumed umber, a small amount of quinacridone fuchsia, and to accomplish this. Titanium white, consumed umber, quinacridone red, and ultramarine blue were utilized in the cloud shadow regions. While using quinacridone red uncovered as an essential worry that it is strong regions for a so you should simply recollect this for little totals. Expecting that you find you have added an abundance of quinacridone fuchsia to your mix you can kill it using cobalt blue-green or turquoise light. Cobalt greenish blue is a greenish blue, so green part will kill the quinacridone fuchsia since it is the variety's free inverse (allude to the combination wheel).

Stage 3: Next I have painted the cliffs in the background. I've used de-sprinkled colors to create lighter tones because I need to make the pretends seem important because they are so far away. The shadow locale of the slants were mixed using a blend of ultramarine blue, consumed umber, quinacridone red and titanium white. Yellow oxide, ultramarine blue, consumed umber, and titanium white were used to blend the lighter grass areas that are both green and yellow. These were completely consolidated as one in evolving degrees. Review you want to keep your assortments de-inundated while painting distant landforms, for instance, slopes and fakes, etc so it gives its presence being far away. If the assortment were unnecessarily sprayed, the imaginative creation's experience slopes would appear more unquestionable and require significance. Quick tip: Avoid using cadmium tones and pthalo green when painting distant landforms because they are unnecessary submerged. After that, I started baffling in Lion Rock with a mix of titanium white, consumed umber, quinacridone fuchsia, and ultramarine blue. I used a mix of consumed umber, consumed sienna, titanium white, and a dab of ultramarine blue for the featured locales. The shadow areas have been made using identical tones however much less titanium white and more ultramarine blue. I need to trick you into feeling that Lion Rock is nearer to me than the bluffs, yet that it is additionally far away from the front's breaking waves. As I have begun to build the immersion of the varieties, there is currently more variety in tone, with light tones becoming lighter and dim tones becoming hazier. My shadow regions show up altogether more dull than the slants behind the scenes since I utilized less titanium white in those areas. I have added a limited quantity of ultramarine blue to all of my consumed umber and consumed sienna mixes to ensure that they are not excessively drenched and introduced excessively far.

Step 4: Next I have begun to paint the foliage on Lion Rock. I've mixed titanium white, ultramarine blue, cobalt blue, consumed sienna, and yellow oxide in various combinations. Precisely when I was painting the foliage, I expected to review that Lion Rock is in the painting. While mixing your greens, start by mixing yellow oxide (also known as yellow ochre) with titanium white, ultramarine blue, and titanium dioxide. If necessary, add some cadmium yellow large and, if necessary, some pthalo green. Be extraordinarily wary while using pthalo green as it is solid locales for amazingly can quickly overpower your mix. A nice early phase is to blend mask greens with yellow oxide and cobalt blue. Enduring I find my greens are too drenched I can pound it back with its free reverse tone, either cadmium red or quinacridone maroon.

Step 5: I have begun painting the sensible wave and the ocean, which should be painted first. I have begun to consolidate more held colors the sea using a blend of ultramarine blue, pthalo green, consumed umber and titanium white. Survey pthalo green has important strong areas for very, but if used in large quantities, it can be overwhelming, so be careful. You can decrease the submersion of the mixes by mixing to some degree consumed umber to the mix which influences the gathering. I have outlined the condition of the stones on the shadow areas of Lion Rock using ultramarine blue and consumed umber with a little degree of titanium white. I utilized titanium white and a little extent of cadmium yellow to appear of the breaking wave. Turquoise light can also be utilized as opposed to cobalt blue-green. By adding some ultramarine blue, you can increase the force of the blue and, if necessary, decrease its submergence by adding some consumed umber. Adding a restricted amount of pthalo green to your blue mix in like manner gives it a green-blue ocean tone. You could have to play with the groupings a piece. Since it will require extra layers once it is dry, I have utilized straight titanium white to approach the highlighted region at the breaking wave's lip as of now.

Step 6: Next I have started to paint the white-water in the forward looking region and foam on the breaking waves. I have used fluctuating blends of ultramarine blue, consumed umber, quinacridone fuchsia and titanium white.

Step 7: I have deterred in the stones in the nearer view using a blend of consumed umber, consumed sienna and yellow oxide and a little titanium white for the highlighted locale. The area where the stones are disguised is painted with consumed umber and ultramarine blue. Exactly when these assortments are obliged they essentially make faint, for this ongoing circumstance I have held the mix to an outstandingly dull brown. Before I start encouraging the subtleties, I let the construction dry after the ruining structure has been finished. Since I have spread out a base to work from I light to fire developing the detail in the imagines and sky. I have begun to describe the mists' shape and refine them. For the highlighted district of the fogs I have added a particularly little degree of yellow oxide with titanium white. This is generally brilliant on the grounds that titanium white is excessively cool right out of the chamber. Warming it up with scarcely enough yellow oxide or yellow ochre will help. However yellow oxide is somewhat more novel than yellow ochre, you can similarly incorporate yellow ochre as opposed to yellow oxide. From there on out, I chipped away at the paint and the disagreeable rocks' detail by adding basically more detail to Lion Rock. I have used a mix of consumed umber, consumed sienna, yellow oxide, titanium white and ultramarine blue. Since Lion Rock is in the painting, I have calmed and semi-desiderated the variety so it doesn't stand isolated extravagantly and battle with the breaking wave in the forward looking locale. I have widened that splashing of my greens on Lion Rock again not quite far. I earthed it with some consumed sienna and a blend of titanium white, yellow oxide, and ultramarine blue. I have added a couple of parts in the foliage and extended the splashing by adding a little cadmium yellow basic and a little degree of pthalo green. Go irrefutably clear with the pthalo green as it's an especially amazing mix and will quickly overpower everything. If you find your green mix is too splashed you can pound the assortment back by adding a free talk like a cadmium red or quinacridone red.

Step 8: I began dealing with the focal region of the craftsmanship, where you can see the undeniable breaking wave from a nearer point. With a round brush, I started to refine the brutal water of the breaking wave and managed the nuances of the highlighted pieces. Again I have added a little yellow oxide with titanium white for the highlighted district of the break wave. The cirrus hazes above have been added by me.

Step 9: Happening with developing the nuances of the breaking waves I have started painting the foam plans in the wave. Keep in mind that the wave obscures the light source, which radiates from behind it. Consequently, I used a mix of titanium white, a little quinacridone fuchsia, and ultramarine blue, and I wiped out the submersion with an ideal extent of consumed umber. I have used liberal degrees of liquin to deal with the stream and I have used a liner brush to achieve the spidery foam plans. I have painted some reflected light in shadow region of the breaking wave by mixing ultramarine blue, quinacridone maroon, sensibly consumed umber and titanium white. I have used really more quinacridone fuchsia to warm up the white-water. Expecting that it gets unreasonably doused with quinacridone fuchsia, I can drench it with cobalt greenish blue to cover it up.

Step 10: For the white water in the center, I used a mix of titanium white, cobalt greenish blue, quinacridone fuchsia, drank umber, and ultramarine blue in varying totals, dependent upon whether I was painting the white water's shadow district or the warm reflected light. Again I have used titanium white mixed in with a yellow oxide for the highlighted region of the white water. I have added more parts to the stones using a mix of yellow oxide, consumed sienna, consumed umber and titanium white. I have likewise introduced the spills on the rocks.

Step 11: (Last Step) To complete the convincing work of art, I have added my different highlights and ramifications for portray the show of the wild sea in this magnum opus. Using an enormous round bristle brush I have mixed titanium white with truly yellow ochre and a liberal degree of liquin I have brushed over the lip of the breaking waves and the white water to give the dubiousness of shower tumbling off the fierce water. Using a commensurate assortment mix I have added further highlights to the nearer view rocks giving them the presence of wet shakes that are reflecting the fast sun. Finally I have added a covering of titanium white mixed in with truly ultramarine blue, quinacridone red and consumed umber to smooth the fogs some spot distant. Liberal proportions of liquin were used to apply this.

CHAPTER THREE

THE BEST TECHNIQUE TO PAINT A DUSK - ACRYLIC SEASCAPE PAINTING SYSTEM

Painting Materials

For this work of art, we'll use these assortment paints: key yellow, titanium white, incredible red, and bewildering blue. Also, these brushes will be utilized: a Purdy house painter's brush, a little fine detail sable brush, a medium level fiber brush, and a fan brush.

Stage 1: Expand the Skyline Line and Pick a Situation for Your Viewpoint Line In this case, we will situate it in the material's base third. Does whatever it takes not to put the horizon line in your fine art in light of the fact that doing so will make it watch out of equilibrium and to an extreme. Utilizing a ruler and a pencil, leave a light etching. Then, use a circle plan and draw in the sun. Since we actually made the horizon line "slanted", placing the sun in the middle is alright.

Stage 2: Paint In Orange Sky Make an orange tone for the sky by mixing the red, yellow, and white paints. Use the enormous painter's brush to put a layer of this orange above locale. Use the edge of the brush while inclining toward the skyline line and the sun's edge for more imperative precision.

Stage 3: Fill In The Sun Acknowledge that the sky will dry preceding occurring with this step, so you can avoid the amaze that we made. Wet the brush a spot by diving it into a water to dial down the orange assortment we actually got on there. Then, using level brush strokes use that tone to fill in the sun's place of combination. White paint ought to be utilized to feature the sun along the top edge starting there on. Allow the orange and white paint to mix together. This will withdraw the sun from the orange sky and give it some division.

Stage 4: Paint In Blue Ocean; For the ocean, we will make a blue gathering using a blend of white and a spot of blue. The blue will provide our organization with a fair qualification because it is comparable to the orange. Once more, use the enormous brush to evenly cover the sea area, but leave a small area under the sun unpainted. We will use this area to paint the sun's appearance in the water. Award your material to dry completely going prior to advancing forward.

Stage 5: Apply the second coat to the sky. After you have washed your brush, we will get back to our astonishing sky tone, which is a base of yellow with a sprinkle of red. Put a hazier shade of orange at the main quality of the sky to give it some segment. Right when we add division to a material or drawing, we give it more perspective. From that point forward, add a little water to your brush to level out the variety and cover the sun with an orange layer. Again, from there on out, dunk the brush in unadulterated white and apply the sun's edge.

Stage 6: The subsequent coat should be applied to the sea. Get your brush clean. Right now we will put on a second for the ocean using a really hazier blue tone than the focal coat. Use long, level brush strokes and let the brush give the paint an unequal appearance. We truly need to get the improvement in the sea since it isn't absolutely quiet and smooth. After that, use flat bungle strokes and a white wash to add a few light dashes of features to the sea.

Stage 7: Paint the Sun's Appearance, Change to the medium level fiber brush and dunk it in some white. Consume free space under the sun for express level strokes. Permit the white paint to blend in with the ocean blue a little. Let this dry eventually before proceeding to the next step.

Stage 8: Keep on going Coat On Sky and Sun; At last we will put our third and keep on going coat on the sky. The sky gets a little bit more lavish with each coat, and more of the material is covered up so that there are no white spots on the other side. Put some white and yellow with a dash of red on your brush and mix it a little on the degree (at this moment not really) and sometime later put a few even strokes above near the sun locale. Permit the paint to mix on the veritable material. We can utilize this to make entrancing runs with various tones. The white we mixed in will back off the sky a ton. This will be a portrayal of concealed, distant mists. We'll involve a blend of white and yellow for the sun, covering the edge with a layer of white/yellow prior to allowing it to turn a light orange as we draw nearer to the middle. What's more, all in all, we'll take the paint that is currently on the brush and placed a couple of highlights in the sun's appearance and the ocean. Permit the work of art to dry.

Stage 9: The Sun and Sea feature switch to the fan brush. Utilize a light orange and feature the sea with level features. These wills represent the orange that comes from the sun and the sky bubbling in the water. It will give our material a very shinny look. After that, using the fan brush, add some white detail to the sun and the sea.

Stage 10: Add A couple of Distant Seagulls; By and by, take your little detail brush and with some faint blue paint, put some "upside down V's" above. These will be a couple of seagulls flying in the distant. Change up the size, circumstance, and number of the seagulls to make crafted by workmanship truly intriguing.

Avoid even amounts of seagulls or setting them too equitably.

TIPS FOR FLEDGLINGS IN SEASCAPE PAINTING

The seascape can be challenging to paint. Water is unusual normally and has clear and wise qualities which can be a misery to make due. I'll give you a couple of pointers to assist you with painting seascapes well here. These are centered on fledgling skilled workers, but further created experts may in like manner feel that they are helpful.

1. Catch the Seascape Token

2. Construct the Seascape's Design

3. Fathom How to Paint Reflected Light

4. Make use of broken variety

5. Hard and delicate edges

6. Match Your Brushwork to the Possibility of the Seascape

7. Make Congeniality Using Typical Tones

Get the Badge of the Seascape

Signal in workmanship conventionally suggests the badge of the human body. But I like to think that the seascape also has a signal that shows how the water moves in general in a rhythmic way. Without signals, your seascape painting could end up looking mechanical and disengaged. I see many undertakings at the model crashing wave seascape, where the wave looks ran onto the rest of the ocean rather than an expansion of it. To get the badge of the seascape, consider what the water would look like if you could use a single line to paint it. This line will address the most fundamental badge of the seascape. You can then use this line to foster plan and design.

Develop the Plan of the Seascape

Correspondingly similarly as with movement, the seascape has an overall development that you should endeavor to get. This development may be fundamental or intricate, dependent upon the kind of seascape you are painting. A very important structure will be found in a tranquil seascape with polished water. You are essentially painting a level surface. A brutal seascape during a whirlwind will have a seriously confounding development as the water cuts and beats. Have a go at isolating the subject into boxes, chambers, and circles. You can paint anything with these shapes, including seascapes.

Learn How to Paint Mirrored Light

Water typically possesses some intelligence, so some light will pass through it. This swaying light shows up in the water. Dependent upon the quietness of the water, the reflections could be an ideal portrayal of the sky above or a broke impression of broken assortment. A method for painting exact reflections is to use more dark lights and lighter darks. So the lights will not be solid areas for as the darks won't be essentially pretty much as significant as the sky (or whatever is being reflected).

Use Broken Variety

The messed-up variety method is ideal for capturing water's clear and intelligent nature. It moreover allows you to foster some charming surface for the water. Despite the fact that it might give the idea that way from a good ways, the sea isn't only one strong variety assuming that you look carefully. On a crisp morning, you will probably see a variety of blues, greens, yellows, and purples. During the sunset, you will probably see different reds, oranges, yellows, and purples. The destroyed assortment technique incorporates using unblended strokes of obvious tones. These assortments could be immovably related (light blue and dull blue) or absolutely interesting (red and green). It's implied that the sort of seascape you are painting will direct the varieties you use. The astonishing show-stopper under by Claude Monet is a phenomenal representation of broken assortment. Here is a close by of the water to give you an unrivaled look at all the wrecked assortment. Notice how insignificant cutting off is done by Monet. Without the rest of the material, this part is by all accounts simply a disaster area of broken assortment. Be that as it may, step back and everything gets together.

Sensitive and Hard Edges

You truly need to give mindful thought to such edges you use in your seascape painting. An overview of the various edges available to you is as follows:

Hard edge: The two shapes undergo a radical transformation.

Fragile edge: A smooth advancement between two shapes.

Lost edge: An advancement between two shapes that is sensitive so much that you can barely see it.

The majority of the edges in artwork depicting seascapes will be fragile or missing. This is in light of the fact that water is certainly not an unbendable development and there is commonly a fragile advancement beginning with one district of the water then onto the following. Regardless, two or three distinctly situated hard edges can have a colossal impact among generally fragile and lost edges.

The following are a couple of legitimate spots for hard edges:

• The most noteworthy place of a crashing wave.

• On a bright day, the skyline line that isolates the sky and the ocean. On a shady or stormy day, a fragile edge may be more reasonable.

• The edge what secludes the sensible water and white foam.

Match Your Brushwork to the Possibility of the Seascape

Here is a general tip that I consider to be particularly useful for seascape painting. Endeavor to match your brushwork to the possibility of the seascape. Take, for instance, the scenario in which you are painting the violent influxes of the oceans and attempt to use broken and misrepresented brushwork. Long, even strokes are best if you're painting the still water of a morning seascape. By doing this, you will foster a surface that matches the seascape you are painting. The seascape's motion and structure will also be built up by the single strokes. Tip: Mix up your brushwork to give your artwork a refined touch of distinction. A tranquil seascape could have little areas of unsettling influence where you can add solid areas for some (like where the water is breaking on the shore). A story seascape could have calm districts between the crashing waves where you can add some more unnoticeable brushwork.

Make Agreeableness Using Typical Tones

In seascape painting, the water will grant various typical tones to the sky in view of reflected light. Subsequently, I will as often as possible jump all around between the water and the sky to guarantee there are ordinary tones used for the two locales. Let's say I'm painting the features on the white, fluttering mists that hang above me. I could take these light tones and use them to paint the whitewash on top of the water. I could take the light blues from the sensible sky and use them to change it up contrast to the water. I can utilize lighter shades of a portion of the water's dim greens and blues to make the mists.

I do a lot of this kind of forward and backward work while painting seascapes. Using comparable tones, the outcome is regularly amicability.

THE END

www.ingramcontent.com/pod-product-compliance
Lightning Source LLC
Chambersburg PA
CBHW071001290526
45795CB00005B/1731